Common Core Lessons & Activities:
Colonial America

By Carole Marsh

Published by Gallopade International, Inc.

Printed in the U.S.A. (Peachtree City, Georgia)

TABLE OF CONTENTS

G: Includes Graphic Organizer

GO: Graphic Organizer is also available 8½" x 11" online download at www.gallopade.com/client/go (numbers above correspond to the graphic organizer numbers online)

READING INFORMATIONAL TEXT

The Lost Colony

Read the text and answer the questions.

In 1587, about 115 people sailed across the Atlantic Ocean from England to America. Their goal was to start the first permanent English colony in the New World. They settled on Roanoke Island, off the coast of what is now North Carolina. However, the colony did not last. In fact, what happened to the colonists is a great mystery.

While establishing their settlement, it did not take the colonists long to realize they needed more food and tools. They urged John White, the colony governor, to return to England to acquire the supplies. White left his wife, daughter, and baby granddaughter behind. He planned to return as quickly as possible.

Unfortunately, when White arrived in England, a war broke out between England and Spain. Queen Elizabeth I decided that all available ships should battle the Spanish fleet and protect England. It was impossible for White to return to Roanoke right away. It was three years before he returned to the colony.

In August 1590, White finally set foot on Roanoke Island again. After all that time, he probably thought he would find a prospering colony. He didn't. Every man, woman, and child was gone. The colony had simply vanished. Only two clues were left behind. One was the word "Croatoan" carved into a post. The other was the letters "CRO" carved into a tree. "Croatoan" was the name of a nearby island. It was also the name of a Native American tribe. Sadly, White was unable to locate the missing colonists.

What happened to the colonists at Roanoke remains a mystery. That is why Roanoke is known as "The Lost Colony."

1. A. What is a synonym for acquire, as it is used in the text?
   B. Use a dictionary or other reference to define prospering.
2. Predict what might have happened to the Roanoke colonists. Go online to find additional ideas. Share your findings with the class.
3. Imagine you are Governor John White. Write two journal entries: one for the day you first arrived at Roanoke, and one for the day you returned three years later.

PRIMARY SOURCE ANALYSIS

James Fort at Jamestown

Look at the drawing and answer the questions.

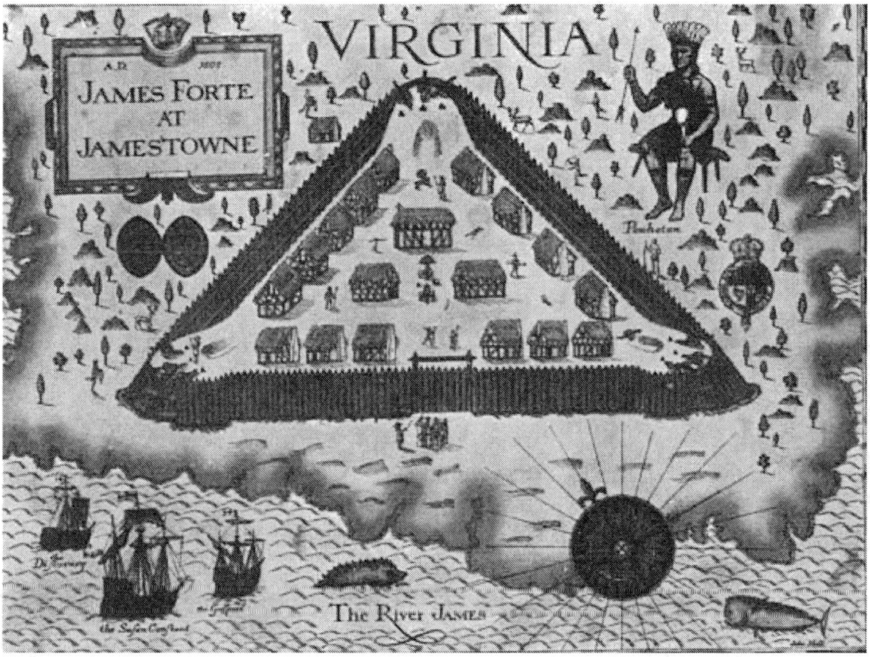

Courtesy of Library of Congress

1. A. What is the first thing you notice about the drawing? Why?
   B. List 3-5 additional observations about the drawing.
2. According to the drawing, what things could be found in and near the fort?
3. Why might the artist have included Chief Powhatan in the drawing?
4. In your opinion, was this a good location for the colonists to construct the fort? List 3-5 reasons to support your answer.
5. The first buildings constructed in the fort were the public buildings, like a storehouse, church, and guardhouse. Explain why colonists constructed those buildings first.

Founding Plymouth Colony

Read the text and answer the questions.

In September 1620, about 100 people boarded a ship in England called the Mayflower. Known as "Pilgrims," they set sail for the New World.

Many Pilgrims sought freedom of religion. They broke ties with the Church of England so they could worship freely. Others hoped to earn money or build a better life. On board the ship, the Pilgrims lived in cramped, dirty, dark conditions. They endured sickness, stormy weather, and damage to their ship.

While crossing the Atlantic, 41 men signed the Mayflower Compact. This document formed the colony's government. It also bound everyone to follow its laws. It was the first document of its kind in the United States.

After two months, the Pilgrims arrived in what is now Massachusetts. They founded Plymouth Colony. Life at Plymouth Colony was difficult. The Pilgrims found it nearly impossible to raise crops in the sandy soil. As provisions ran low, they could not replenish their food supply. Also, their shelters provided little protection against the biting cold. During their first winter, more than half of the settlers died from hunger or disease.

Fortunately, the colonists were befriended by the Wampanoag, a Native American people. The Wampanoag taught the Pilgrims to hunt, fish, gather fruit, and raise corn and other crops. The Pilgrims and Wampanoag had a strong friendship for many years.

1. A. Infer the meaning of the phrase broke ties, as it is used in the text.
   B. Explain the meaning of replenish, as it is used in the text.
2. How did the Mayflower Compact affect the lives of the Pilgrims?
3. Predict what might have happened if the Pilgrims had not met the Wampanoag. Cite evidence from the text to support your answer.
4. Imagine you are a Pilgrim child and you make friends with a Wampanoag boy or girl. Write a narrative about an experience you have together at Plymouth Colony.

PRIMARY SOURCE ANALYSIS

Early Savannah

This is an 18th century illustration of Savannah, Georgia. Analyze the illustration and answer the questions.

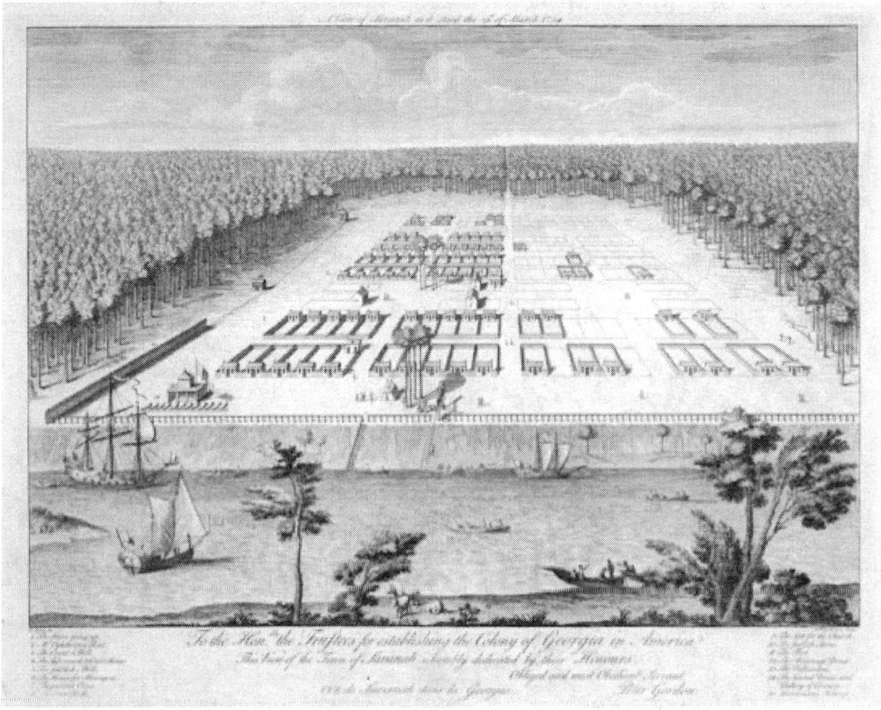

Courtesy of Library of Congress

1. A. Why was this location a good choice to build a city?
   B. Do you think there were any drawbacks to this location? Cite evidence from the illustration to support your answer.
2. Infer how Savannah might have looked 10 years before this illustration was drawn. Predict how it looked ten years after.
3. In your opinion, who was the most likely audience for this image?
4. Divide into groups. Use online resources to learn why Savannah was built in squares. Do the squares still exist today? Create a computer presentation using old drawings and newer drawings/photos of the city. Present your research to the class and discuss.

MAP ACTIVITY

The 13 Colonies

Look at the map and answer the questions.

Major Products of the Colonies (Early 1700s)

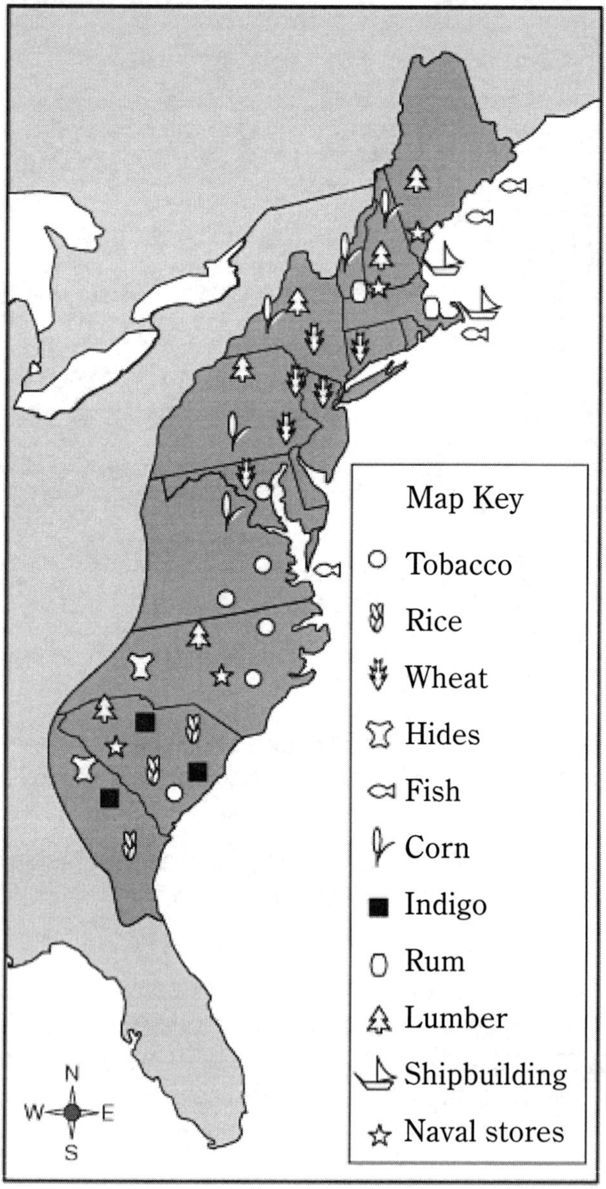

PART A: Follow the instructions to label the map.

1. Circle the New England colonies in blue. Circle the Middle Colonies in green. Circle the Southern colonies in red.
2. Using classroom or other resources, make a list of the colonies in each region.
3. Label each colony on the map.

PART B: Use a dictionary and the map to answer the questions.

4. Define <u>naval stores</u>. Which region produced them?
5. Define <u>hides</u>, as used on the map key. Which region produced them?

PART C: Answer the questions.

6. Infer what occupations were common in the New England colonies.
7. What products were most commonly grown in the Middle Colonies?
8. Which important "cash crop" grew in most of the Southern colonies? Describe a cash crop in your own words.

PART D: Complete the activities.

9. What is indigo? Divide into groups and use online or classroom resources to research the product and its importance in colonial times. Create a computer presentation to present to the class.
10. Compare and contrast colonial products. Re-create the graphic organizer below. Label one circle for each of the three groups of colonies. Use the map and map key to complete the graphic organizer.

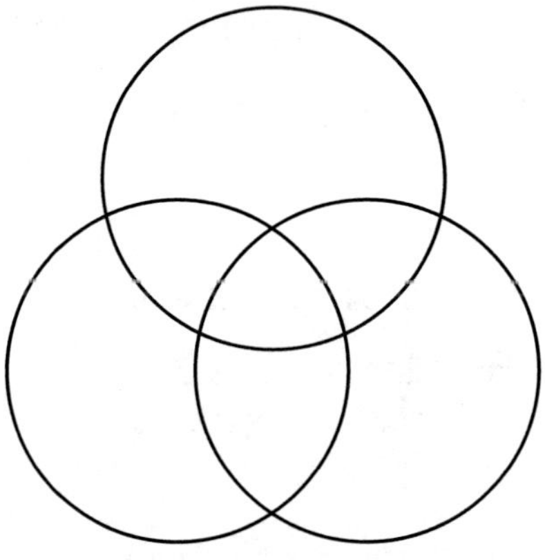

Settling Pennsylvania

Read the text and answer the questions.

In the 17th century, English citizens were expected to worship under the Church of England. William Penn, an Englishman, disagreed. His feelings were so strong that he founded his own colony.

Penn was raised with the beliefs of the Church of England. However, he began speaking out against the church while he was a college student. At age 22, he met some Quakers in Ireland. Quakers are peace-loving and oppose war. They are sometimes known as "Friends." Penn liked their ideas. He became a Quaker.

Penn was a leader in the Quaker community. As a result, he was selected to found a Quaker settlement in the British colonies. In 1677, King Charles II gave him land west and south of what is now New Jersey. Penn would act as governor. That year, 200 English Quakers sailed to the Province of Pennsylvania. Penn wrote the new colony's laws. He granted people freedom of religion and free elections of their leaders. He also guaranteed fair trials and freedom from being wrongly put in jail. These ideas would later form the foundation of the U.S. Constitution. Like the Pilgrims, Penn formed friendships with the Native Americans.

Pennsylvania's policy of religious freedom attracted many people from Europe. More Quakers arrived from other countries. Protestants, Lutherans, and Amish came as well. All could worship as they chose. Pennsylvania became their haven. The new colony was a success.

1. Use a dictionary or other reference to define haven.
2. A. Describe the beliefs of the Quakers.
   B. Why do you think Quakers are sometimes called "Friends"?
3. How was William Penn similar to the Pilgrims?
4. How did William Penn influence the laws of the United States?
5. Create a poster that illustrates the ideas Pennsylvania was founded upon. Present your poster to the class.

PRIMARY SOURCE ANALYSIS

Colonial Quotations

Rewrite each quotation to complete the chart. Use the completed chart to answer the questions.

Quotations:	**Rewrite quotations in your own words:**
"If We allow Slaves, we act against the very Principles by which we associated together, which was to relieve the distressed." — James Oglethorpe	
"I expect to pass through this world but once. Any good therefore that I can do, or any kindness or abilities that I can show to any fellow creature, let me do it now. Let me not defer it or neglect it, for I shall not pass this way again." — William Penn	
"We must delight in each other, make others' conditions our own, rejoice together, mourn together, labor and suffer together, always having before our eyes our commission and community in the work, our community as members of the same body." — John Winthrop	

1. Use a dictionary or other reference to find a synonym for defer.
2. Who are the speakers? Use online research to write a short biography of each speaker. What do all three speakers have in common? Proofread and edit your work.
3. Summarize the common theme shared by all three quotations.
4. Predict how a Southern plantation owner might react to James Oglethorpe's quote.

PRIMARY SOURCE ANALYSIS

Join, or Die

This 1754 political cartoon shows the American colonies as a snake divided into segments. Analyze the cartoon and answer the questions.

Courtesy of Library of Congress

1. A. What is the main idea conveyed in this cartoon?
   B. Do you think the phrase "Join, or Die" is necessary to convey this idea? Explain.
2. Who is the intended audience of this cartoon? How do you know?
3. List each abbreviation in the cartoon and the colony it represents. (N.E. stands for New England. Be sure to list the New England colonies.) Locate each on a modern-day map of the United States.
4. Which two colonies are not included in the snake? Research why.
5. Based on the ideas in this cartoon, draw your own political cartoon about colonial unity. Present your cartoon to the class. Discuss how students' cartoons are similar and different.

Colonial Vocabulary

Use a dictionary and other resources to complete the graphic organizer for each vocabulary word.

Vocabulary:

- apprentice
- cash crop
- charter
- export
- governor
- import
- indentured servant
- indigo
- naval stores
- plantation
- settlement
- tradesman

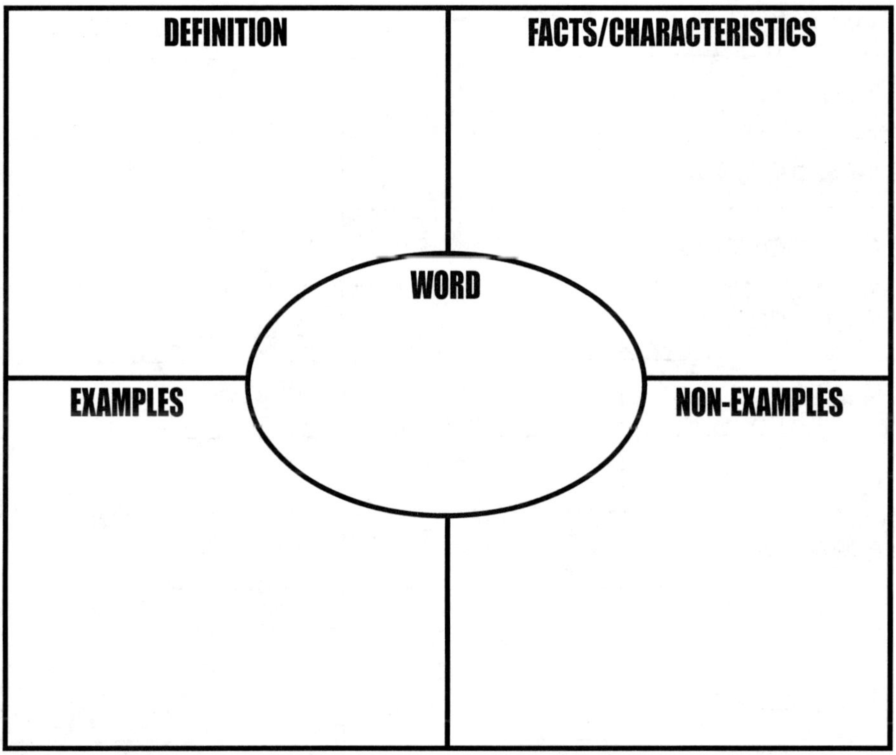

Compare and Contrast the 13 Colonies

Use online or classroom resources to complete the graphic organizer. List the sources you used.

Colony	Year Founded	Founded By
Connecticut		
Delaware		
Georgia		
Maryland		
Massachusetts		
New Hampshire		
New Jersey		
New York		
North Carolina		
Pennsylvania		
Rhode Island		
South Carolina		
Virginia		

Region	Major Products/Industries

Plantation Economy

Read the text and answer the questions.

In Colonial America, plantations became the foundation of the Southern economy.

Plantations were vast tracts of land. Some stretched for thousands of acres. The Southern soil and climate allowed the land to flourish with crops that could not grow elsewhere. Virginia was famous for its tobacco. Cotton became a major crop in Georgia and Mississippi. South Carolina grew both cotton and rice.

Most of these crops were not used by the people who raised them. They were known as "cash crops" because they were shipped out of the South and sold for money. Most cash crops were shipped to northern states and Europe. Cotton was especially popular. It was sent to mills to be turned into fabric. In addition, Virginia's tobacco was in high demand because smoking was popular in England. People around the world relied on Southern plantations' crops. Plantation owners charged high prices for what they grew. As a result, their profits grew as well.

To have a thriving plantation, owners needed many workers. They bought slaves to plant, tend, and harvest their crops, among other chores. On the largest plantations, it was common to see hundreds of slaves toiling in the fields. Since slaves were forced to work long hours without pay, they provided the cheapest source of labor. Plantations relied heavily on their slaves to produce these important crops.

Southern plantations thrived until the 1860s, when slavery ended. After that, plantation life changed forever.

1. A. Define foundation, as it is used in the text.
   B. Explain the meaning of tracts, as it is used in the text.
   C. Give a synonym and an antonym for flourish.
2. How were cash crops different from other kinds of crops?
3. Why could plantation owners charge high prices for their crops?
4. Predict how plantations might have been different if owners were not allowed to have slaves.

Slaves vs. Indentured Servants

Use the graphic organizer to compare and contrast the lives of slaves and indentured servants.

Slaves

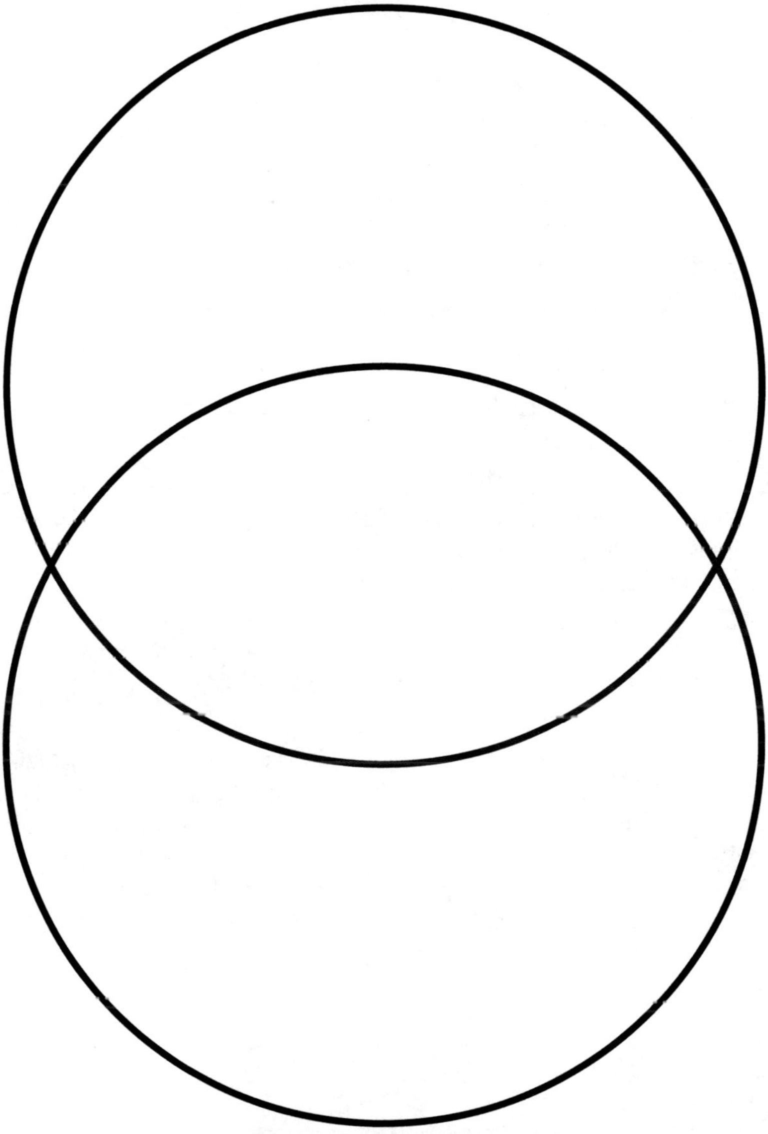

Indentured Servants

Mercantilism and Triangular Trade

Read the text and look at the map. Then answer the questions on the next page.

By the mid-1700s, several colonial towns had grown into large cities. Examples were New York City, Boston, and Charleston. The reason these cities grew was because of trade. These cities all had natural harbors where ships could come in to unload and pick up goods for trade.

At that time, many ships involved in trade followed a route between Britain and the colonies. The British government believed that one of the main purposes of the colonies was to supply goods to England. This was part of a concept known as mercantilism.

The goal of mercantilism was for Britain to gain wealth by controlling trade from its colonies. The British government wanted the colonies to ship raw materials to Britain, where they were used to manufacture goods. In turn, Britain wanted the colonies (and other countries) to buy manufactured goods from them.

Many cargo ships traveled along routes across the Atlantic Ocean that became known as "triangular trade" routes. These routes were made easier by wind and sea patterns in the Atlantic Ocean. In the 1400s, people had learned that winds and sea currents moved in a circular pattern over the northern Atlantic Ocean. Because ships used sails, this was important information. Sailors navigated their vessels into the currents.

The "triangular trade" system consisted of three main trade routes. The routes linked Britain, the British colonies, and Africa as points of a triangle across the Atlantic. Trade was centered around three main things. The first was raw materials, like tobacco, sugar, or cotton from the colonies. The second was manufactured products like textiles, furniture, and guns from Britain. The third was slaves from Africa to provide free labor to raise crops in the New World.

Basic Triangular Trade Routes

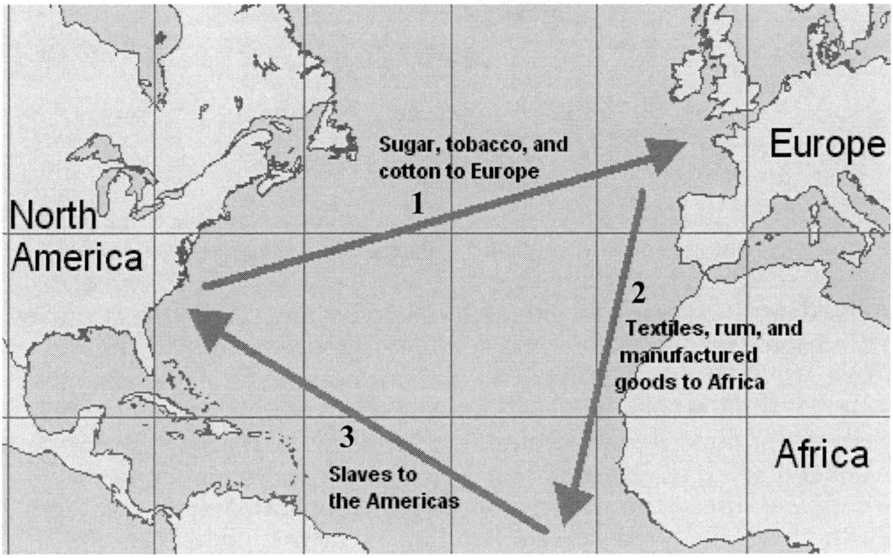

1. A. Use a dictionary or other reference to define <u>currents</u>.
   B. What is the meaning of <u>circular</u> as it is used in the text?
   C. What is a synonym for <u>navigate</u>?
2. Find New York City, Boston, Philadelphia, and Charleston on a map of the United States. What do they have in common regarding trade in colonial times?
3. Who benefited most from mercantilism? Cite evidence from the text and map to support your answer.
4. How did nature contribute to the success of triangular trade?
5. What is the difference between raw and manufactured goods? Give examples in your answer.
6. Explain the role of each route on the map in the system of triangular trade.
7. Draw your own triangular trade map based on the one above. Use online or classroom resources to find other goods that were shipped along the three trade routes. Add each to the correct route.
8. Use online resources to research what factors led to the end of the triangular trade system. Write a paragraph to explain why.

PRIMARY SOURCE ANALYSIS

Journal of Edward Winslow

Read the text by Edward Winslow, a Plymouth colonist, and answer the questions.

"Our harvest being gotten in, our governor sent four men on fowling, that so we might after a special manner rejoice together, after we had gathered the fruit of our labors; they four in one day killed as much fowl, as with a little help beside, served the company almost a week, at which time amongst other recreations, we exercised our arms, many of the Indians coming amongst us, and among the rest their greatest King Massasoit, with some ninety men, whom for three days we entertained and feasted, and they went out and killed five deer, which they brought to the plantation and bestowed on our governor, and upon the captain, and others. And although it be not always so plentiful, as it was at this time with us, yet by the goodness of God, we are so far from want that we often wish you partakers of our plenty."

—December 1621

1. A. Infer the meaning of fowling.
   B. Explain the phrase fruit of our labors.
   C. Use a dictionary or other reference to define bestowed. What is a synonym for the word?
2. What is the mood of the text? Use logical reasoning to support your answer.
3. Summarize Edward Winslow's writing. What is the main idea of the text?
4. List 3-5 words to describe the condition of Plymouth Colony.
5. What does the phrase "yet by the goodness of God" tell you about Winslow?
6. How are the Pilgrims and Native Americans similar?
7. What can you infer about the feelings between the Pilgrims and Native Americans at the time this text was written? Cite evidence from the text to support your answer.

SECONDARY SOURCE ANALYSIS

Feast at Plymouth Colony

Look at the painting and answer the questions.

Courtesy of Wikimedia Commons

1. What historic event is shown in this painting? Cite evidence from the painting and the text on page 18 to support your answer.
2. Describe the mood of the painting. Cite evidence from the painting to support your answer.
3. This painting was created in 1914. Why is it a secondary source, not a primary source?
4. A. What is the role of the person marked with Arrow 1?
   B. What does the presence of this person tell you about life in colonial America?
5. Write a journal entry from the perspective of one of the children in the foreground of the painting. Be sure to include sights, sounds, tastes, and smells to describe the event.
6. Who is identified by Arrow 2? Use the text on page 18 to identify who one of the Native Americans might be.

Colonial Trades and Occupations

Read the text and answer the questions.

Settlements in the colonies with skilled tradesmen had a good chance of success. Each trained person helped the settlement and its people to survive.

One of the most valuable people in colonial times was the blacksmith. A blacksmith worked with iron. He forged and repaired items like axe heads and hammers.

Chandlers were also important. They made candles. Without candles, colonists could not have done much after the sun set.

Gunsmiths were needed to make and repair guns. For their trade, they learned to work with wood and iron. Without properly working guns, colonists would have had a very limited food supply.

Coopers used wood to make containers such as barrels. Barrels stored gunpowder, tobacco, flour, and other valuable items. A poorly made barrel could be a disaster for a family or merchant.

Wheelwrights made and fixed wagon and carriage wheels. They worked with both wood and iron. Sturdy wheels were needed on rough, dirt roads. Without them, shipping goods would have been impossible.

Each trade in colonial America was unique and necessary. Hardworking skilled tradesmen allowed colonial settlements to grow and prosper.

1. Use a dictionary to define forge.
2. What are some other items a blacksmith might have made or fixed?
3. Infer why a poorly made barrel would be harmful.
4. How were gunsmiths and wheelwrights similar?
5. Predict what might happen if a settlement lost its wheelwright.
6. In your opinion, what was the most important job in colonial America? Explain your choice with logical reasoning.

Colonial America Events

Put these events in chronological order on the graphic organizer. Compare your chart with your classmates' charts.

Colonists arrive on Roanoke Island	The city of Savannah is founded	The Wampanoag help the Pilgrims	The Calverts found Maryland	The *Mayflower* leaves England
American Revolution begins	The Pennsylvania colony is settled	James Fort is built	Tobacco is first grown in Virginia	John White returns to Roanoke

Colonial America Events:

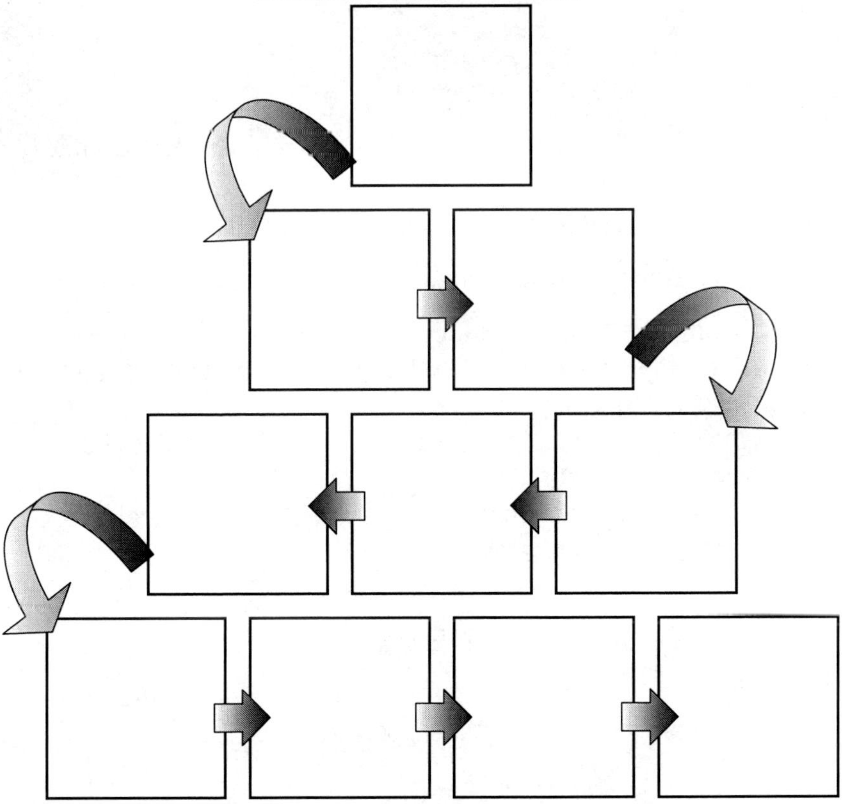

Slave Auction

This is a 19th century engraving of a slave auction in South Carolina. Analyze the engraving and answer the questions.

Courtesy of Wikimedia Commons

1. What is the main idea conveyed in this engraving?
2. How is the setting significant to the engraving's message?
3. Identify who is represented in the engraving:
   A. Who is the person marked with arrow A? Which details from the engraving support your answer?
   B. Who is the person marked with arrow B? Which details from the engraving support your answer?
   C. Who are the people marked with arrow C? Which details from the engraving support your answer?
4. What are the words on the flag? Do they support or oppose the action taking place in the engraving? Explain.
5. What can you infer about the person who created this engraving? Cite evidence from the engraving to support your conclusions.

6. How might the following people have reacted to this engraving?
   A. a plantation owner
   B. a politician
   C. a slave

7. Working in groups, go online to find political cartoons depicting slavery during the 19th century. Compare the ideas in the image on page 22 with others you find. Prepare a computer presentation of the images you collect. Discuss your findings in class.

BONUS: Compare this source with Plantation Economy on page 14. What can you conclude about the overall opinion of people in the South in regard to slavery?

BONUS: Draw the graphic organizer below. In the Problem box, write: Growing cotton requires lots of workers. Then, complete the organizer from the perspective of a plantation owner.

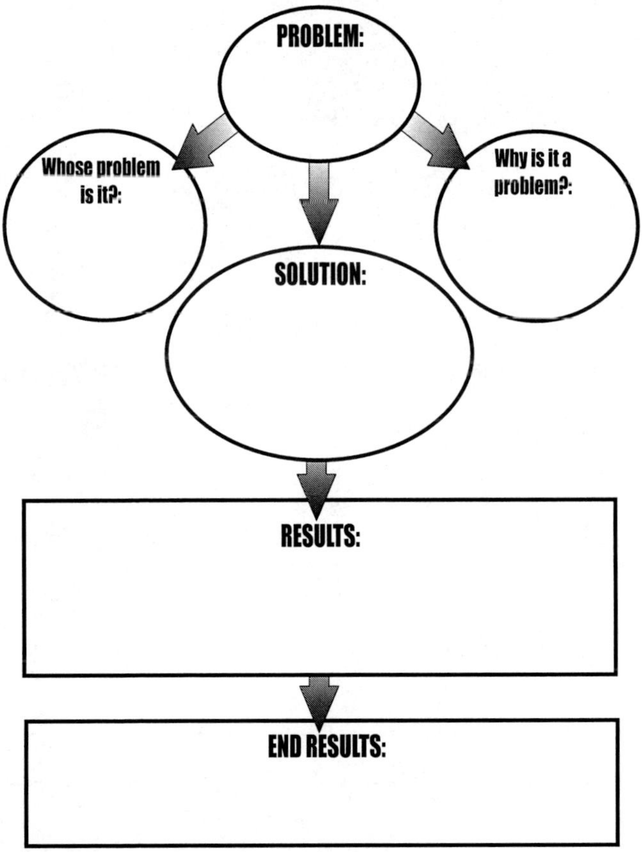

Correlations to Common Core State Standards

For your convenience, correlations are listed page-by-page and for the entire book!

This book is correlated to the Common Core State Standards for English Language Arts grades 3-8, and to Common Core State Standards for Literacy in History, Science, & Technological Subjects grades 6-8.

Correlations are highlighted in gray.

PAGE #	READING *Includes:* RI: Reading Informational Text RH: Reading History	WRITING *Includes:* W: Writing WHST: Writing History, Science, & Technology	LANGUAGE *Includes:* L: Language LF: Language Foundational Skills	SPEAKING & LISTENING *Includes:* SL: Speaking & Listening
2	RI/RH · **1** 2 **3** **4** 5 6 7 8 9 **10**	W/WHST · 1 2 **3** **4** 5 6 **7** 8 **9** **10**	L/LF · 1 2 3 **4** **5** **6**	SL · **1** 2 3 **4** 5 6
3	RI/RH · 1 2 3 4 5 6 **7** 8 9 **10**	W/WHST · **1** **2** 3 4 5 6 7 8 9 **10**	L/LF · 1 2 3 4 5 6	SL · 1 2 3 4 5 6
4	RI/RH · **1** 2 **3** **4** 5 6 7 **8** 9 **10**	W/WHST · 1 2 **3** **4** 5 6 7 8 **9** **10**	L/LF · 1 2 3 **4** 5 **6**	SL · 1 2 3 4 5 6
5	RI/RH · 1 2 3 4 5 6 **7** 8 9 10	W/WHST · 1 2 **3** **4** 5 **6** **7** 8 9 **10**	L/LF · 1 2 3 4 5 6	SL · **1** 2 3 **4** **5** **6**
6-7	RI/RH · 1 2 3 4 5 6 **7** 8 **9** **10**	W/WHST · 1 **2** **3** 4 5 **6** **7** 8 9 **10**	L/LF · 1 2 3 **4** 5 **6**	SL · **1** **2** 3 **4** **5** 6
8	RI/RH · **1** 2 3 **4** 5 6 7 **8** 9 **10**	W/WHST · 1 **2** 3 **4** 5 6 7 8 9 **10**	L/LF · 1 2 **3** **4** 5 **6**	SL · 1 2 3 **4** **5** **6**
9	RI/RH · **1** 2 3 **4** 5 **6** **7** 8 **9** **10**	W/WHST · **1** 2 3 **4** **5** 6 **7** **8** **9** **10**	L/LF · 1 2 3 4 **5** 6	SL · 1 2 3 4 5 6
10	RI/RH · **1** **2** **3** 4 5 6 **7** 8 9 10	W/WHST · 1 **2** 3 **4** 5 6 **7** 8 9 **10**	L/LF · 1 2 3 4 **5** **6**	SL · **1** 2 3 **4** **5** 6
11	RI/RH · 1 2 3 **4** 5 6 7 8 9 **10**	W/WHST · 1 2 3 4 5 6 7 8 9 10	L/LF · 1 2 3 **4** 5 **6**	SL · 1 2 3 4 5 6
12-13	RI/RH · 1 2 3 **4** 5 6 **7** 8 9 **10**	W/WHST · 1 2 3 4 5 6 **7** **8** 9 10	L/LF · 1 2 3 4 5 6	SL · 1 2 3 4 5 6
14	RI/RH · **1** 2 3 **4** **5** 6 7 **8** 9 **10**	W/WHST · **1** 2 3 **4** 5 6 7 8 9 **10**	L/LF · 1 2 3 **4** **5** **6**	SL · 1 2 3 4 5 6
15	RI/RH · 1 2 3 4 5 6 **7** 8 **9** **10**	W/WHST · 1 2 3 **4** 5 6 7 **8** **9** **10**	L/LF · 1 2 3 4 5 **6**	SL · 1 2 3 4 5 6
16-17	RI/RH · **1** 2 **3** **4** **5** **6** **7** **8** **9** **10**	W/WHST · 1 **2** 3 **4** 5 6 **7** 8 9 **10**	L/LF · 1 2 3 **4** **5** **6**	SL · 1 2 3 4 5 6
18	RI/RH · **1** **2** **3** **4** 5 6 7 **8** 9 **10**	W/WHST · 1 **2** 3 **4** 5 6 7 8 **9** **10**	L/LF · 1 2 3 **4** **5** **6**	SL · 1 2 3 4 5 6
19	RI/RH · 1 2 3 4 **5** 6 **7** 8 9 10	W/WHST · 1 2 3 4 5 6 7 8 9 10	L/LF · 1 2 3 4 5 6	SL · 1 2 3 4 5 6
20	RI/RH · **1** 2 3 **4** 5 6 7 **8** 9 **10**	W/WHST · **1** **2** 3 **4** 5 6 7 8 **9** **10**	L/LF · 1 2 3 4 **5** **6**	SL · 1 2 3 4 5 6
21	RI/RH · 1 2 3 4 **5** 6 **7** 8 9 10	W/WHST · 1 2 3 4 5 6 **7** 8 9 10	L/LF · 1 2 3 4 5 **6**	SL · **1** 2 3 4 5 6
22-23	RI/RH · 1 **2** **3** 4 **5** **6** **7** **8** 9 **10**	W/WHST · 1 2 3 **4** 5 **6** **7** 8 **9** **10**	L/LF · 1 2 **3** 4 5 **6**	SL · **1** **2** 3 **4** **5** **6**
COMPLETE BOOK	RI/RH · **1** **2** **3** **4** **5** **6** **7** **8** **9** **10**	W/WHST · **1** **2** **3** **4** **5** **6** **7** **8** **9** **10**	L/LF · 1 2 **3** **4** **5** **6**	SL · **1** **2** 3 **4** **5** **6**

For the complete Common Core standard identifier, combine your grade + "." + letter code above + "." + number code above.

In addition to the correlations indicated here, the activities may be adapted or expanded to align to additional standards and to meet the diverse needs of your unique students!